Backyard Animals

Deer

Christine Webster

www.av2books.com

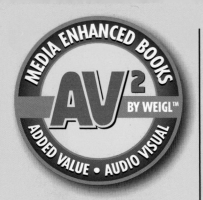

AV² provides enriched content that supplements and complements this book. Weigl's AV² books strive to create inspired learning and engage young minds in a total learning experience.

Your AV² Media Enhanced books come alive with...

 Audio
Listen to sections of the book read aloud.

 Video
Watch informative video clips.

 Embedded Weblinks
Gain additional information for research.

 Try This!
Complete activities and hands-on experiments.

 Key Words
Study vocabulary, and complete a matching word activity.

 Quizzes
Test your knowledge.

 Slide Show
View images and captions, and prepare a presentation.

... and much, much more!

Go to www.av2books.com, and enter this book's unique code.

BOOK CODE

Q862810

AV² by Weigl brings you media enhanced books that support active learning.

Published by AV² by Weigl
350 5th Avenue, 59th Floor
New York, NY 10118
Website: www.av2books.com   www.weigl.com

Library of Congress Cataloging-in-Publication Data

Webster, Christine.
 Deer / Christine Webster.
    p. cm. -- (Backyard animals)
 Includes index.
 ISBN 978-1-61913-066-1 (hard cover : alk. paper) -- ISBN 978-1-61913-263-4 (soft cover : alk. paper)
 1. Deer--Juvenile literature. I. Title.
 QL737.U55W38 2013
 599.65--dc23
                        2011044652

Printed in the United States of America in North Mankato, Minnesota
1 2 3 4 5 6 7 8 9 0 16 15 14 13 12

WEP060112
012012

Project Coordinator Karen Durrie
Art Director Terry Paulhus

Every reasonable effort has been made to trace ownership and to obtain permission to reprint copyright material. The publishers would be pleased to have any errors or omissions brought to their attention so that they may be corrected in subsequent printings.

Photo Credits
Weigl acknowledges Getty Images as its primary photo supplier for this title.

Contents

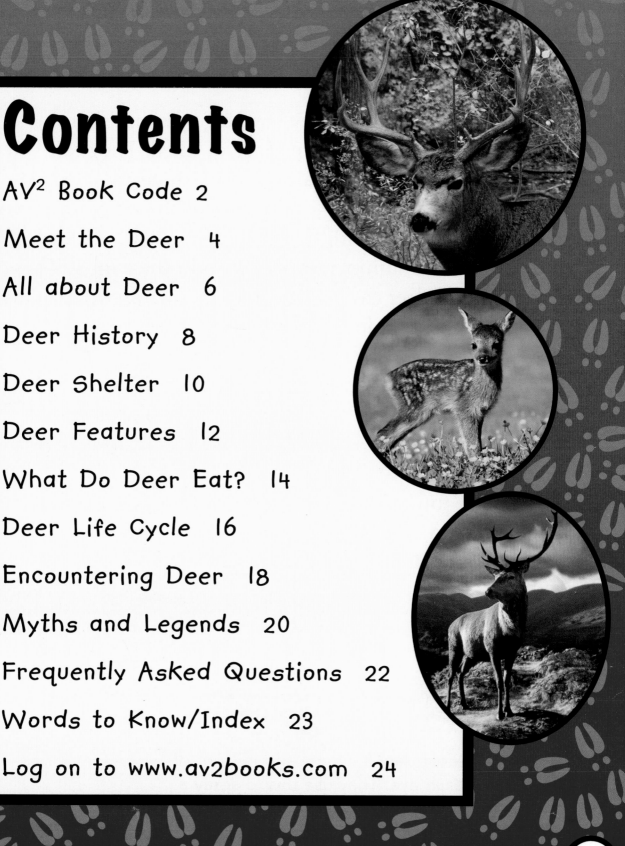

Meet the Deer

Deer are **mammals**. They have big eyes and sharp hearing. Deer have a keen sense of smell. They can run very fast, and they are good swimmers.

Deer are covered with fur. The fur is usually reddish-brown in the summer. It is grayish in the winter. These colors let a deer easily blend into its surroundings. This helps the deer hide from **predators**.

Male deer are called bucks. Bucks have **antlers** on their heads. Female deer are called does. Most does do not have antlers.

Deer are found in North America, Europe, northern Africa, and Asia. They live in open meadows, mountains, forests, and swamps.

Most deer have a gland in front of each eye. They use this to spray a smelly scent where they live and eat.

Deer can run as fast as 36 miles (58 kilometers) per hour.

All about Deer

There are more than 30 deer **species**. Each species has special features. Deer are the only animals with antlers on their heads.

Some deer species, such as the Chinese water deer, are very small. The smallest deer is the South American pudu. It is only 10 inches (25 centimeters) high at the shoulder. Other species, such as the moose, are quite big.

Often, only male deer grow antlers. In some species, such as caribou, both males and females grow antlers.

Sizes of Deer

American Elk
- Weighs 650 pounds (295 kilograms) to 1,000 pounds (454 kg)

Caribou
- Males weigh 275 pounds (125 kg) to 660 pounds (300 kg)

Chinese Water Deer
- Weight ranges from 200 pounds (91 kg) to 300 pounds (136 kg)

Moose
- Largest member of the deer family
- Males can weigh up to 1,800 pounds (816 kg)

Mule Deer
- Weighs 110 pounds (50 kg) to 475 pounds (215 kg)

White-tailed Deer
- Weighs 150 to 300 pounds (68 to 136 kg)

Deer History

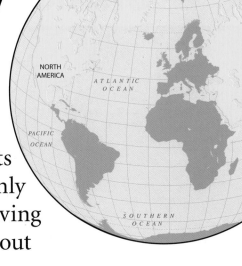

Deer have been on Earth for millions of years. The first deer appeared in Asia about 38 million years ago. Scientists believe that deer once lived only in Arctic areas. They began living in parts of North America about 4 million years ago.

The deer's biggest threats were animal predators. These included wolves and mountain lions. Humans also hunted deer as a food source.

Today, humans are the deer's main predator. Humans hunt deer for many reasons. Deer are hunted for their meat, or venison. Their skin can be used as clothing.

Fascinating Facts

The Irish elk has not lived on Earth since 5000 B.C. This giant animal stood 7 feet tall (2.1 m) at the shoulder. Its antlers measured more than 12 feet (3.7 m) across.

Mule deer are sometimes called black-tailed deer. This is because they have a black-tipped tail.

Deer Shelter

Most deer live in forests or near grassy meadows. They rest on the ground. The place where they rest is called a deer bed. Deer look for places that are surrounded by tall grasses, plants, trees, and shrubs. This protects them from harsh weather, such as rain or snow. It also hides them from predators. A deer bed is about 4 feet (1.2 m) long and 1.5 feet (0.5 m) wide.

Some deer, such as caribou, travel from place to place with the changing seasons. This is called migration.

Male deer mark their territory by stomping on the ground and making scrape marks in the dirt. They may rub their antlers on trees. This is called a buck rub.

Some species of deer live in forests. Others live near water.

Deer Features

A deer's body is adapted to offer protection from predators. Strong legs allow deer to leap 9-foot (2.7-m) fences. They can swim 13 miles (21 km) per hour. The color of their fur helps deer hide well in forests. Every part of a deer's body is well adapted to its surroundings.

EYES
Deer have large eyes on both sides of their head. This allows them to see in front and behind without moving their head.

NOSE
A deer's sense of smell is much more sensitive than a human's. A deer's nose has membranes that capture scents easily. Membranes are thin layers of skin tissue.

TEETH
Deer teeth are made to chew tough food, such as plants. Deer have **incisors** that allow them to bite. **Molars** help deer grind their food into smaller pieces.

EARS
Deer have large ears. They can hear very well. Deer ears rotate, or turn, acting like **radar**. They pick up sounds quickly.

COAT
A deer's coat acts as **camouflage.** In the summer, it is reddish-brown to blend in with the leaves on trees. In the winter, it is grayish-brown, so it blends in with the bare forests.

What Do Deer Eat?

Deer are herbivores. This means they eat plants, such as herbs, leaves, and grass. Deer choose foods that can be easily **digested**. In the summer, they graze on leaves, grass, alfalfa, wheat, berries, acorns, and herbs. During the winter, deer eat twigs, wildflowers, nuts, and fruits. They will **scavenge** corn, wheat, and soybeans from farmers' fields.

A deer's stomach has four chambers to help digest this food more easily. In the first chamber, acids break down the tough plant fibers. Later, the deer will cough up the food. The deer will chew the food again, and then swallow it. The food then passes through the other three stomach chambers.

Scientists can tell the age of a deer by looking at its teeth. Chewing tough food wears down its teeth. Older deer will have shorter teeth.

Deer are often fearful of predators. This causes them to eat their food quickly.

Deer Life Cycle

The deer's mating season is called a rut. Bucks will fight for their territory during this time. Males will crash their antlers against one another to claim females.

Birth

At birth, a white-tailed fawn has a reddish coat with white spots. It weighs from 3 pounds (1.4 kg) to 7 pounds (3.2 kg). Shortly after birth, the doe quickly licks the fawn clean. This is so predators do not smell its scent. Fawns take a step within 20 minutes after being born.

1 Day to 5 Months

The mother hides the fawn in the grass for one week. This allows the baby time to grow strong. During this time, the fawn nibbles on plants and drinks its mother's milk. At six weeks, fawns stop drinking their mother's milk. Their spots fade after about five months.

A doe is pregnant for five to ten months. Does give birth in May or June. Baby deer are called fawns or calves. A doe can have one to three fawns.

Adult

Female fawns may stay with their mother for two years. Males often leave after a year. At this time, they are considered to be adults. They are ready to live on their own.

Encountering Deer

Often, a doe will leave her fawns for hours at a time while she finds food. Most times, she will return. A doe will not come for her fawn if a human is nearby. It is best to leave the area without touching the fawn.

If a fawn is injured or ill, call a wildlife officer for help. The fawn may need to be moved to a safe place. Ask an adult to gently put the animal in a cardboard box. Pad the box with towels and blankets. The fawn may be scared and upset. It is important not to touch or talk to the fawn. The fawn can have water to drink. Do not give it food. The wildlife officer will know how to help the fawn.

Fascinating Facts

When a white-tailed deer senses danger, it raises its tail. This is called "flagging." Flagging may serve as a warning signal to other deer and to let a predator know it has been seen.

People often see deer while hiking through natural areas. Hikers should not feed or touch the animals.

Myths and Legends

People all over the world have myths about deer. Deer are very important to the Huichol people of Mexico. They believe the deer is the symbol of Kayumahli. He is a guide and guardian that only shamans can hear. Shamans are spiritual guides.

The Huichol believed their ancestors came from wolves. The Huichol would hunt deer and offer the animal's blood to the gods or goddesses. This allowed the Huichol to remain human.

The red stag appears in old northern European myths. Stories feature kings and other rich people trying to match wits with swift and clever stags.

How the Deer Got His Antlers

Here is a retold legend passed down by Cherokee Indians.

Deer had no antlers, but he was a fast runner. His friend Rabbit was a great jumper. The animals in the forest wanted to know who could travel the fastest. Rabbit and Deer agreed to race. The winner would receive a pair of antlers.

Rabbit and Deer were to race through a thicket, turn, and come back. Before they began, Rabbit said, "I don't know this part of the country. I want to take a look through the bushes to see where to run."

Rabbit went into the thicket. He was gone so long that the other animals became worried. They sent someone to look for him. Rabbit was found gnawing on bushes to clear a path. The messenger told the other animals. Rabbit was accused of cheating. They gave the antlers to Deer. He has worn them ever since.

Frequently Asked Questions

Do deer grow new antlers each year?

Answer: Bucks shed their antlers each year. They grow new antlers in the summer. If they have plenty of healthy food, their antlers will grow bigger each year.

What do deer tracks look like?

Answer: Deer have hoofs. These are like toenails. Hoofs make a heart-shaped track on the ground. The pointed part of a track shows which way a deer is traveling.

What do deer sound like?

Answer: Deer make many sounds. A white-tailed fawn looking for its mother will bleat like a sheep. An injured white-tailed deer will bawl. This is a long, loud, high-pitched call. All deer make snorting sounds.

Words to Know

antlers: bony growths on a deer's head

camouflage: to blend in

digested: to be broken down in the stomach into substances that can be used by the body

incisors: front teeth used for cutting and gnawing

mammals: animals that have fur, make milk, and are born alive

molars: back teeth that have a broad grinding surface

predators: animals that hunt other animals for food

radar: an instrument that bounces radio waves off unseen objects to find out where they are located, how fast they are moving, and in what direction they are traveling

scavenge: to take something usable from discarded material

species: a group of living things that has many features in common

Index

Log on to www.av2books.com

AV² by Weigl brings you media enhanced books that support active learning. Go to www.av2books.com, and enter the special code found on page 2 of this book. You will gain access to enriched and enhanced content that supplements and complements this book. Content includes video, audio, weblinks, quizzes, a slide show, and activities.

Audio
Listen to sections of the book read aloud.

Video
Watch informative video clips.

Embedded Weblinks
Gain additional information for research.

Try This!
Complete activities and hands-on experiments.

WHAT'S ONLINE?

Try This!	Embedded Weblinks	Video	EXTRA FEATURES
Identify different types of deer.	Find more information on deer identification.	Watch a video about deer behavior.	**Audio** Listen to sections of the book read aloud.
List important features of the deer.	Learn more about the history of deer.	See a deer in its natural environment.	**Key Words** Study vocabulary, and complete a matching word activity.
Compare the similarities and differences between young and adult deer.	Complete an interactive activity.		**Slide Show** View images and captions, and prepare a presentation.
Test your knowledge of deer.	Discover more about encountering deer.		**Quizzes** Test your knowledge.
	Read more stories and legends.		

AV² was built to bridge the gap between print and digital. We encourage you to tell us what you like and what you want to see in the future.

Sign up to be an AV² Ambassador at www.av2books.com/ambassador.